I Wonder Why

Mountains Have Snow on Top

and other questions about mountains

Jackie Gaff

KINGFISHER

BOSTON

KINGFISHER
a Houghton Mifflin Company imprint
222 Berkeley Street
Boston, Massachusetts 02116
www.houghtonmifflinbooks.com

First published in hardcover in 2001
First published in this format in 2004
10 9 8 7 6 5 4 3 2 1
1TR/0204/SHE/RNB/126.6MA(F)

LIBRARY OF CONGRESS CATALOGING-IN-PUBLICATION DATA
has been applied for.

ISBN 0-7534-5763-6

Printed in Taiwan

Series designer: David West Children's Books
Author: Jackie Gaff
Consultant: Keith Lye
Illustrations: James Field (SGA) 20t, 22–23, 24t;
Mike Lacey (SGA) 4, 8–9, 20b, 21t, 23b, 24–25,
26–27, 28b, 29, 30; Sean Milne 18–19; Liz Sawyer
(SGA) 16–17, 19b; Stephen Sweet (SGA) 6–7, 8t;
Mike Taylor (SGA) 12–13; Ross Walton (SGA) 5,
10–11, 14–15, 28–29, 30–31; Peter Wilkes (SGA)
    all cartoons.

CONTENTS

What's the difference between a mountain and a hill?

Mountains are larger than hills, and mountainsides are often steep and difficult to climb—unlike a hill's gentle slopes. Some experts say that if a peak is over 2,000 feet (600m) higher than the surrounding land, then it is a mountain. Any less, it is a hill.

● A molehill is a tiny pile of soil that, like a mountain, sticks up from the surrounding land.

● About one fourth of all land on Earth is mountainous.

• A row of mountains is called a range.

Can spacecraft measure mountains?

Radar equipment measures mountains by bouncing sound signals off the ground. Machines record the time the signals take to bounce back, then use this to work out how high the mountain is. The radar is carried on board high-flying airplanes and space satellites.

• The top of a mountain is called its peak or summit.

• Even though a mountain may be far from the sea, its height is measured as the distance above the sea's surface—sea level.

Where is the world's highest mountain?

The highest place in the whole world is at the top of Mount Everest. This huge mountain is in the Himalayan ranges of central Asia, and it rises to 29,021 feet (8,848m) above sea level.

NORTH AMERICA

SOUTH AMERICA

ATLANTIC OCEAN

Alaska Range

Rocky Mountains

Appalachians

Sierra Nevada

Andes

● Although only 13,792 feet (4,205m) of Mauna Kea sticks up above sea level, this Hawaiian mountain is even taller than Everest. From its base on the ocean floor to its peak, it is an amazing 33,465 feet (10,203m).

● The world's longest mountain range on land is the Andes in South America, at about 4,450 miles (7,200km) long.

Famous mountains

1 McKinley (U.S.)
20,320 ft.

2 Logan (Canada)
19,850 ft.

3 Whitney (U.S.)
14,494 ft.

4 Popocatépetl (Mexico)
17,930 ft.

5 Cotopaxi (Ecuador)
19,347 ft.

6 Aconcagua (Argentina)
22,834 ft.

7 Kilimanjaro (Tanzania)
19,340 ft.

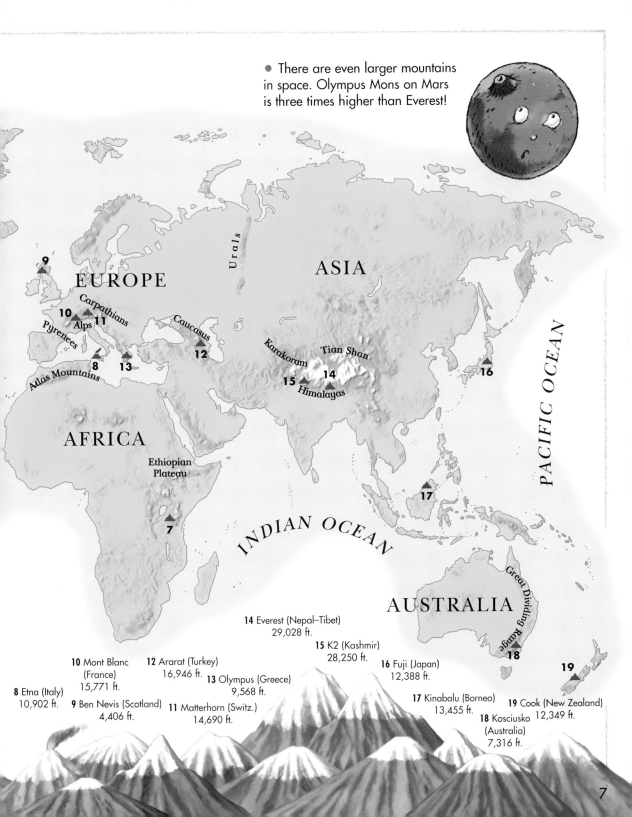

● There are even larger mountains in space. Olympus Mons on Mars is three times higher than Everest!

EUROPE

ASIA

Urals

Carpathians

10 Alps 11

Pyrenees

Caucasus

12

Karakoram

Tian Shan

Atlas Mountains

8   13

14

15 Himalayas

16

PACIFIC OCEAN

AFRICA

Ethiopian Plateau

7

INDIAN OCEAN

17

AUSTRALIA

Great Dividing Range

18

19

9

14 Everest (Nepal–Tibet) 29,028 ft.

15 K2 (Kashmir) 28,250 ft.

10 Mont Blanc (France) 15,771 ft.

12 Ararat (Turkey) 16,946 ft.

13 Olympus (Greece) 9,568 ft.

16 Fuji (Japan) 12,388 ft.

8 Etna (Italy) 10,902 ft.

9 Ben Nevis (Scotland) 4,406 ft.

11 Matterhorn (Switz.) 14,690 ft.

17 Kinabalu (Borneo) 13,455 ft.

18 Kosciusko (Australia) 7,316 ft.

19 Cook (New Zealand) 12,349 ft.

7

Do mountains move?

They certainly do! Earth
is a bit like a giant, round
egg, with a shell called the
crust, then a layer called
the mantle, and a core in
the middle. The crust is cracked, like
an eggshell, and is made from about
30 gigantic pieces, called plates. The plates
float around very slowly on top of the mantle,
which is partly melted and flows like molasses.

Crust

Mantle

Core

● The plates that carry
North America and Europe
are floating apart by about
1.5 inches (4cm) each year.

How do mountains form?

● Volcanoes are openings
in Earth's crust where fiery clouds
of hot ash, gas, and red-hot liquid
rock, called lava, spit out. Most
volcanic mountains form when
lava and ash cool into layer
upon layer of solid rock.

Although the plates that make up
Earth's crust move incredibly slowly,
their movements are powerful enough
to make mountains. Different movements
give birth to the three main types of
mountains—volcanic, block, and fold.

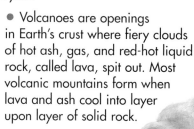

Why do some mountains have pointed tops?

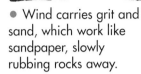

Even while a mountain is forming, the weather, ice, and flowing water start to wear it away and carve its top into sharp points. The wearing away is called erosion.

● Wind carries grit and sand, which work like sandpaper, slowly rubbing rocks away.

● Block mountains form when part of the crust is squeezed up between two cracks called faults.

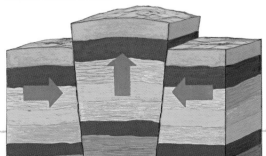

● Fold mountains form as two plates slowly crunch into each other, pushing the crust up into bumps and loops.

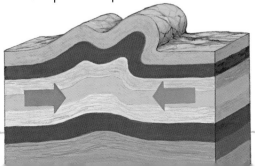

9

Why do volcanoes blow their tops?

A volcano begins deep inside the Earth as bubbles of gas and liquid rock called magma. This mixture slowly rises because it is lighter than the solid rock around it. As it pushes its way up, it gets squashed and squeezed. The pressure keeps building up, until the gas and magma explode through a weak place in Earth's crust—making the volcano erupt and blow its top.

● The effect of gas and magma erupting from a volcano is like what happens when you shake a soft-drink bottle and then take off the cap.

● When magma hits the surface, it is called lava.

• The ancient Romans believed a god of fire lived beneath a volcanic island off the coast of Italy. They called this god Vulcanus—that's where our word "volcano" comes from.

Are all volcanoes dangerous?

There are three main types of volcanoes, and they can all be dangerous. Active volcanoes erupt fairly often. Dormant volcanoes sleep quietly for years but erupt every now and then. Extinct volcanoes have stopped erupting and probably won't erupt again—

if we're lucky!

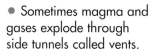

• Sometimes magma and gases explode through side tunnels called vents.

Which was the noisiest volcano?

When Indonesia's Krakatoa blew its top in 1883, the explosion was heard more than an eighth of the way around the world—as far away as central Australia and the west coat of the United States.

Which mountains grow into islands?

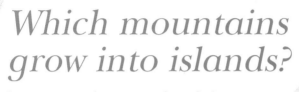

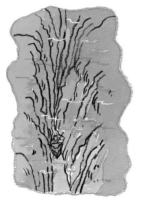

There are thousands of tiny islands dotted through the world's oceans, and most of them were made by volcanoes slowly growing up from the ocean floor.

- With its bottom 36,188 feet (11,033m) below sea level, the world's deepest valley is the Mariana Trench in the Pacific Ocean.

- The world's longest mountain range is nearly all under water. It's called the Mid-Atlantic Ridge, and it stretches for about 9,920 miles (16,000km), from Iceland almost to Antarctica.

Mid-Atlantic Ridge

NORTH AMERICA

EUROPE

SOUTH AMERICA

AFRICA

ATLANTIC OCEAN

Can mountains sink?

Yes. An atoll is a ring-shaped island that can form around the rim of a sunken volcano. The atoll is made from limestone, and the limestone is made by tiny sea creatures called corals.

Lagoon

Coral atoll

● The water in the middle of a coral atoll is called a lagoon.

What are black smokers?

Black smokers are strange chimney stacks that build up on the ocean floor and belch out steamy, black clouds of boiling hot water. All kinds of weird and wonderful animals live near them, including red-and-white worms as long as cars.

Why do mountains have snow on top?

Not all mountains have snow on top, only the highest ones. That's because when water gets very cold, it freezes and turns into snow or ice—and the higher you go up a mountain, the colder it gets. The place where a mountain begins to be covered in snow is called the snow line.

● The higher you go up a mountain, the windier it is. Winds can howl at over 186 mph (300 km/h) at the top of the Himalayas.

● For every 985 feet (300m) you climb up a mountain, the temperature drops by almost 4°F (2°C).

When does snow move as fast as a race car?

Sometimes on high mountains, a mass of snow will suddenly slip and begin to slide downhill. This is an avalanche. The worst avalanches hurtle down like race cars, at more than 100 mph (160km/h).

Can snow move mountains?

Snow and ice can crack and break rocks, slowly wearing away the mountains. The most powerful mountain-movers are glaciers. These massive blocks of ice, snow, and rock form high in the mountains and flow downhill like enormous frozen rivers, carving out valleys.

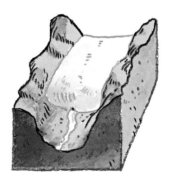

● Glaciers carve out U-shaped valleys. V-shaped valleys are formed by rivers.

Glacier

Why don't plants grow on mountaintops?

The top of a high mountain is one of the coldest, windiest places on Earth, and plants hate it. Plants need water, sunlight, and soil they can get their roots into. Take these things away, and plants give up and die.

● Rivers and melting snow wash soil down off mountaintops, so the higher you go, the thinner the soil is.

Which plants grow on mountainsides?

Large trees can't survive up toward the snow line, but alpines are small, ground-hugging plants that have developed ways of beating the poor soil and bad weather.

● The world's oldest known tree lives in the White Mountains of California. It's a bristlecone pine, and it's already had 4,700 birthdays!

How do mountain plants keep warm?

Some alpine plants, such as edelweiss, have hairy leaves that work like an animal's furry coat to keep them warm. Others, such as gentians, have very dark leaves and flowers, because dark colors attract more of the Sun's warmth than light ones do.

● Plants can't take in water if it is frozen as ice or snow.

● The toughest kinds of trees are conifers, such as pine trees, but even they cannot grow on high slopes.

Which plant can melt snow?

Like many plants, the alpine snowbell disappears under ground in the winter. When new shoots start to push up through the snow in spring, they give off enough heat to melt their way through.

Can animals live on mountains?

Animals find mountain life just as tough as plants do, so most of them stick to the lower slopes. The ones that live higher up have to be good climbers—like mountain sheep, goats, and antelopes.

● The Rocky Mountain goat can climb the steepest cliffs. Hollows under its hooves stick to rock like suction cups, stopping it from slipping.

Which mountain animal has a skirt?

The yak's long, silky hair falls into a skirt around its knees, keeping it warm. This is just as well, because it lives in the highest region in the world—Tibet, in Asia.

How high do birds nest?

Although many birds make flying visits, very few nest high in the mountains. The record-holder is the alpine chough, which nests as high on the slopes as 22,960 feet (7,000m).

● The Andean condor spends its days soaring above the Andes Mountains of South America. Its wings are wide enough for a car to park on!

Which animal became famous for mountain rescues?

● Some people believe that big, hairy, apelike creatures called yetis live in the Himalayas. However, no one has ever proved that yetis really exist.

Saint Bernards are big, clever dogs that are famous for rescuing travelers who lose their way in snowy mountain passes. The dogs were first trained back in the 1600s by monks living in the Alps.

Why do mountain houses have sloping roofs?

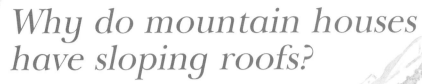

A sloping roof stops too much snow from piling up on top of a mountain house—the extra snow slides off, like a skier sliding down a slope. The parts of the roof that stick out beyond the walls are very wide, too, to keep the falling snow away from the walls.

Why do farmers build steps on mountains?

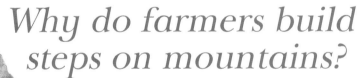

In many parts of the world, mountain farmers build low walls to stop rainwater from washing the soil away. This creates stepped fields, called terraces, where the soil is deep enough for crops to grow.

● Lake Titicaca is too high for many trees to grow, so everything from boats to houses is made out of reeds.

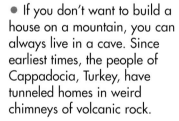

● If you don't want to build a house on a mountain, you can always live in a cave. Since earliest times, the people of Cappadocia, Turkey, have tunneled homes in weird chimneys of volcanic rock.

Who fishes on the world's highest lake?

At 12,503 feet (3,812m) above sea level, Lake Titicaca in Peru, South America, is the highest navigable lake in the world. Local people live on islands in the lake and fish from boats woven from reeds.

● Some mountain rivers are blocked and turned into lakes by a strong, high wall called a dam. The lake water is used to drive machines that generate electricity.

Who built palaces in the mountains?

Back in the 1400s, the Incas ruled over vast parts of the Andes Mountains of South America. They built amazing stone towns and palaces in the mountains, including the mysterious Machu Picchu.

● The Incas were conquered by Spanish invaders in the 1500s. When American explorer Hiram Bingham stumbled across Machu Picchu in 1911, it had been deserted for well over 400 years.

Which monks live in the mountains?

Mount Athos, in Greece, is home to 20 monasteries, and lots and lots of monks. It isn't a single peak. It is a mountainous strip of land that sticks out like a finger from the mainland.

Which city is on top of the world?

Tibet borders the Himalayas. It's so high that people call it the "roof of the world." It's no surprise, then, that the Tibetan city of Lhasa is the world's highest—over 11,800 feet (3,600m) above sea level.

● Even valley bottoms in Tibet are higher than most countries' mountains.

● Women aren't allowed to visit Mount Athos—even female animals are banned!

Who were the mountain men?

American explorers like Kit Carson became known as "mountain men" during the 1800s, because they roamed through the wildest parts of the Rocky Mountains, trapping beavers and other animals for their fur.

When did the first person climb a mountain?

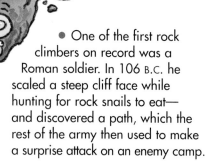

Although people must have been scrambling up high mountains for thousands of years, we only know about the climbers whose stories have been recorded in writing. One of the first recorded mountain climbers was a Japanese monk named En no Shokaku, who made it to the top of Mount Fuji in 633.

● One of the first rock climbers on record was a Roman soldier. In 106 B.C. he scaled a steep cliff face while hunting for rock snails to eat— and discovered a path, which the rest of the army then used to make a surprise attack on an enemy camp.

Who were the first people to climb Mount Everest?

The first people to climb the world's highest mountain were Edmund Hillary of New Zealand and Tenzing Norgay of Nepal. They reached the summit of Everest on May 29, 1953.

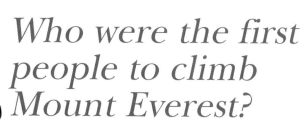

How do people climb mountains?

Climbers use special equipment to help them get up steep rock faces or over slippery ground, and to protect them from falling. Ropes are a climber's lifeline. One end goes around the waist, and the other is looped through metal spikes called pitons, which are hammered into the rock as the climber moves up.

● To get a grip on slippery snow and ice, climbers fix metal spikes called crampons to their boots.

● The first woman to get to the top of Mount Everest was Junko Tabei of Japan, on May 16, 1975.

How do people surf on snow?

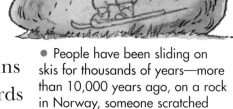

They head for the mountains with a snowboard! Snowboards are a cross between a ski, a surfboard, and a skateboard. When they were first made in the 1960s, they were called "Snurfers."

- People have been sliding on skis for thousands of years—more than 10,000 years ago, on a rock in Norway, someone scratched a picture of a skier.

- Avid snowboarders don't give up when spring comes and the snow melts. They just switch to a new kind of souped-up skateboard—the mountainboard.

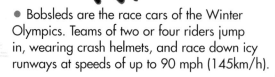

- Bobsleds are the race cars of the Winter Olympics. Teams of two or four riders jump in, wearing crash helmets, and race down icy runways at speeds of up to 90 mph (145km/h).

Who hurtles down mountains faster than an express train?

High-speed trains can go over 125 mph (200km/h), and so can downhill skiers and snowboarders. The skiers are the fastest—the world record is nearly 155 mph (250km/h).

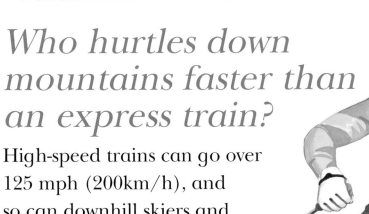

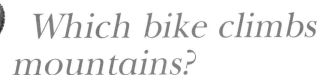

Which bike climbs mountains?

A mountain bike has a lot of gears to help you pedal up steep tracks, and tires with traction for gripping slippery slopes. And if the going gets too tough, you can always get off and carry the bike!

Which is the longest mountain tunnel?

Switzerland is home to some of Europe's highest mountains as well as to the world's longest road tunnel. The St. Gotthard tunnel burrows for just over 10 miles (16km) through the Alps, linking Switzerland to Italy.

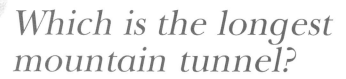

● Over 2,000 years ago, a general called Hannibal led an army and 40 shivering African war elephants over the Alps to attack Rome.

Where is the world's highest railroad?

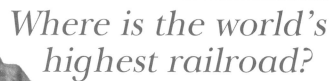

Passengers on the railroad between Lima and Huancayo in Peru, South America, need a good head for heights. The line crosses the Andes Mountains, and the train climbs to over 15,700 feet (4,785m) above sea level.

- To stop them from slipping backward, some mountain trains have three wheels instead of the usual two. The third wheel is in the middle, and it's toothed so it hooks onto a racked track.

Which is the steepest railroad?

The view is fantastic on the Katoomba Scenic Railway in Australia's Blue Mountains, but the ride is pretty hairy. This railroad is the world's steepest, dropping 1,360 feet (415m) in a little under two minutes.

- While you're in South America, jump on the world's longest cable car ride. It runs about 7.5 miles (12km) up into the Andes, from the Venezuelan city of Mérida.

Where is "the great pebble"?

The world's largest rock is a special place for the Aborigines of central Australia, who call it Uluru, meaning "great pebble." Uluru soars nearly 1,141 feet (348m) above the surrounding desert, and measures nearly 6 miles (9km) around its base.

● Uluru glows a brilliant red when the Sun hits it at dawn and dusk. When the sky is cloudy, it looks like the back of a huge, sleeping elephant.

Why do people climb Mount Fuji?

At 12,385 feet (3,776m) high, Mount Fuji is the highest mountain in Japan. It's also one of Japan's holiest places—more than half a million people climb it every year to say their prayers on its summit.

• The ancient Greeks believed that Zeus, the king of their gods, lived in a glittering palace at the top of Mount Olympus. Olympus rises to 9,568 feet (2,917m) and is the highest mountain in Greece.

Which mountain looks like a tabletop?

Table Mountain in South Africa was named because its summit is as flat as a tabletop. It is often covered in clouds, which people call the Tablecloth.

• Africa's highest mountain is Kilimanjaro. At 19,335 feet (5,895m), Kilimanjaro is so high that its top is always covered by snow and ice—even though it's in hot lands, close to the equator.

Index